◀ DRUM EDITION ▶

As recorded by METALLICA on ELEKTRA Records

Management: Q Prime, Inc.
Transcribed by Howard Fields
Edited by Jon Chappell
Music Engraving by W. R. Music
Production Manager: Daniel Rosenbaum
Art Direction: Alisa Hill
Administration: Monica Corton
Director of Music: Mark Phillips

Photography by Ross Halfin

ISBN 978-0-89524-576-2

HAL•LEONARD®

Visit Hal Leonard Online at
www.halleonard.com

Contact us:
Hal Leonard
7777 West Bluemound Road
Milwaukee, WI 53213
Email: info@halleonard.com

In Europe, contact:
Hal Leonard Europe Limited
42 Wigmore Street
Marylebone, London, W1U 2RN
Email: info@halleonardeurope.com

In Australia, contact:
Hal Leonard Australia Pty. Ltd.
4 Lentara Court
Cheltenham, Victoria, 3192 Australia
Email: info@halleonard.com.au

CONTENTS ■ ■ ■ ■ ■ ■ ■ ■ ■ ■

THE DRUM STYLE OF LARS ULRICH

As drummer, songwriter, and founder of Metallica, Lars Ulrich has elevated this unique band to the top of the speed metal thrash pile. Many people consider *Master of Puppets* to be the ultimate classic thrash metal album and Lars Ulrich the leading practitioner of modern thrash metal drumming. Such regaled status in the annals of heavy metal history is a far cry from what might have been for Lars Ulrich.

As a teenager in his native Denmark, Lars, following in his father's footsteps, was actually a top-ten ranked tennis player when he was 16 years old. But in 1973, Lars' long-haired hippie dad took him to a Deep Purple concert in Copenhagen. The next day he ran out and bought his first record, Deep Purple's *Fireball*. This was the beginning of the transformation. Then, in 1980, Lars and his father moved to Los Angeles to promote his tennis career, but it didn't take long for them to realize that Lars' respectable European ranking meant little in the ferociously competitive U.S. tennis circuit. It was then the music took over.

Lars describes the first drum lessons he took in 1980-81 in L.A.: "It didn't add up to much, simply because I never had the patience to deal with that kind of stuff on the level that it should be dealt with, and I was always too excited about playing in a band and just going out and doing it. I could never just sit at home for three hours a night going right, left, left, right. I didn't have the patience for that." So, in 1981, he called up an acquaintance, James Hetfield, who shared his restlessness, pent-up energy and fervor for the likes of Iron Maiden, Def Leppard and Motorhead. With that phone call, Metallica was born. The band played its first gigs in the spring of 1982, only five years after Lars acquired his first drum kit. Since that first kit, the strides that Lars has taken on the drums have done a lot to dispel preconceived ideas as to what can and can't be done on a drum set.

When asked about the flurry of bass drum notes that often fall just before a snare drum backbeat while playing time, Lars commented, "Yeah, that's three on the bass drums, RLR, before the snare hits. My standard, basic thing is to throw in a triplet, and then a snare and a cymbal. That's the standard Lars Ulrich thing...triplets are a precious thing to me. They're a great thing if you know how to throw them in. I started doing the triplets when I first started out on one bass drum, but I learned a couple of years ago that you could get them clearer, and get a lot more punch out of them if you did them on two bass drums."

Throughout *...And Justice for All*, Lars truly establishes himself as "master of triplets." The following lick, taken from the long double-time and guitar solo section of "The Frayed Ends of Sanity" occurs over twenty times in that section and can be found over and over again in different ways, shapes and forms throughout the album. It is an impressive and effective Lars Ulrich stylistic trademark.

"The Frayed Ends of Sanity"
Guitar solo: bars 7 - 8

During the verse of the same song, Lars again inserts this figure, but this time it is against a sixteenth-note hi-hat pattern. Notice how the triplet doesn't begin until the last hi-hat note before the snare hit, hence, a thirty-second note triplet.

"The Frayed Ends of Sanity"
1st, 2nd, 3rd Verses: bar 3
Half time feel

"Dyers Eve" is one of Metallica's fastest songs to date, but this doesn't stop Lars from incorporating the same pattern throughout the song. This time, however, it begins on the downbeat. This excerpt occurs right after the overdubbed tom fill towards the beginning of the song.

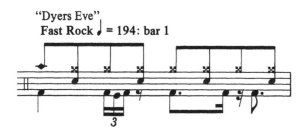

Lars' predilection for bass drum triplets should in no way detract from his ability to sit down behind two bass drums and thunder out classic, machine gun-like sixteenth-note patterns that are so characteristic of the style. He very precisely demonstrates this on "Eye of the Beholder," "Blackened," "The Shortest Straw" and in this excerpt from the verse of "Dyers Eve."

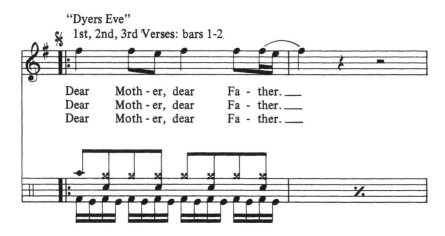

It would be most conspicuous in its absence to discuss Lars Ulrich's double bass playing on *...And Justice for All* and not mention a particular lick that is indeed among the most well liked and impressive. The pattern is the repeating sextuplets that he plays in the section before the long guitar solo that ends the song.

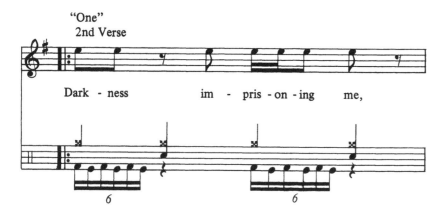

It was interesting and insightful to hear Lars speak of this particular figure: "...I tell you, of all the shit I play on the bass drums live, that's the hardest thing to play tight in the course of a gig. Especially if I'm low on energy, sometimes that shit's all over the place (*laughs*). Obviously, not *that* bad, but I think that section there is the hardest part of the two and a half hours on stage. Most of the time I fly right through it. Any of the stuff I play double bass on, like "Battery" or whatever, I go through that a lot easier because that's just stamina, but this stuff is really difficult because it's got to be really tight and if I'm struggling on an off night, that's the hardest thing to keep together of anything we do live."

Another phenomenal stylistic element of Lars' playing is the mercilessly unrelenting speed at which his hands move when playing time. This is exemplified by songs such as "Blackened," "Dyers Eve," and "The Frayed Ends of Sanity." It was interesting to hear him speak of this. "The only thing I can suggest to people is just do it, and do it, and do it. I don't do anything specific off the kit to do it. I think the best thing you can do is just sit down and practice it. Don't just play fast for the hell of it. I feel very strongly about this. It's gotta have a feel to it. Anyone can just sit down and practice and practice until they can go as fast as humanly possible, and so what? If it doesn't have the feel, I don't think it matters."

Another aspect of Lars Ulrich's drumming is one that is not so much derivative of Lars the player, but of Lars the songwriter. As any avid Metallica listener knows, it's not uncommon for the band to be playing in a 4/4 groove, and then suddenly drop in one bar of the oddest, most *out* time signature, rendering any previous foot tapping pathetically useless. This occurs at various obvious places in "Blackened." Lars perked up when asked about these odd bars and where they come from. "Man, they come from under a rock. You know, me and James write most of the songs together and we don't sit there and try to do this stuff on purpose. We don't say, 'Let's be cool and trendy and come up with the most far-out time signature in the world, and have everybody talk about how great we are.'" He went on to explain how strange musical events like those bars are used as connectors or vehicles to get from point A to point B in a song. "You know, because we fool around with so many tempos and time signatures, the hardest thing we run into is making ends meet, and that's when it becomes fun because that's when you break all the rules."

And indeed he does. When Lars Ulrich plays the drums, he often breaks the rules: of rhythm, of tempo, of meter, and, if you will, of drumming, but in such a rewarding, relevant, musical manner, that it wouldn't make any sense for him to do it more conventionally. Breaking rules has become a way of musical life for Lars Ulrich and Metallica, and it would be criminal for them to stop now.

DRUM SETUP DIAGRAM
LARS ULRICH'S DRUM SETUP

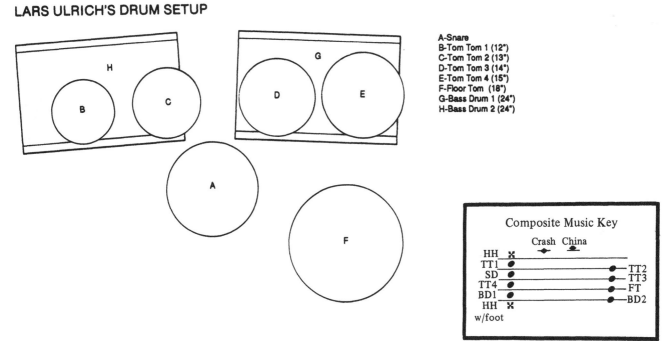

A-Snare
B-Tom Tom 1 (12")
C-Tom Tom 2 (13")
D-Tom Tom 3 (14")
E-Tom Tom 4 (15")
F-Floor Tom (18")
G-Bass Drum 1 (24")
H-Bass Drum 2 (24")

Composite Music Key

DRUM NOTATION EXPLANATION

HI-HAT

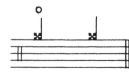

OPEN AND CLOSED HI-HAT: Strike the open hi-hat on notes labeled with an *o*. Strike the closed hi-hat on unlabeled notes.

HI-HAT WITH FOOT: Clap hi-hat cymbals together with foot pedal.

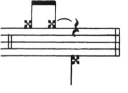

HI-HAT WITH SLUR: The open hi-hat is struck and then closed with the foot on the beat indicated by the hi-hat w/foot notation below, creating a *shoop* sound.

CYMBALS

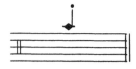

CHOKE: Hit the crash cymbal and catch it immediately with the other hand, producing a short, choked crash sound.

BELL OF CYMBAL: Hit the cymbal near the center, directly on the cup or bell portion.

CYMBAL ROLL: Play a roll on the cymbal rapidly enough to produce a sustained, uninterrupted *shhh* sound lasting for the number of beats indicated.

DRUMS

CROSS STICK: Anchor the tip end of the stick on the snare drum skin at the eight o'clock position, two to three inches from the rim. Then raise and lower the butt end, striking the rim at the two o'clock position, producing a clicky woodblock-type sound.

FLAM: Hit the drum with both sticks, one slightly after the other, producing a single, thick-sounding note.

RUFF: Play the grace notes rapidly and as close to the principal note as possible. The grace notes are unaccented and should be played slightly before the beat. The principal note is accented and played directly on the beat.

CLOSED ROLL: Play a roll on the snare drum creating a sustained, uninterrupted *tshhh* sound lasting for the duration of the rhythm indicated and with no break between the two tied notes.

BLACKENED

Words and Music by
James Hetfield, Lars Ulrich
and Jason Newsted

*2nd time play crash on beat 4.

Chorus

Fill 1

Drum Fig. 1

Dark-est col-or. Blis-tered earth. True death of life._____

Ter-mi - a-tion. Ter-mi - a-tion. Ex-pir-a -tion.
(Ter-mi - a-tion. Ex-pir-a - tion. Can-cel-

Can-cel - la-tion hu-man race. Ex-pec - ta-tion.
la -tion. Ex-pec - ta-tion. Lib-er-

Lib-er - a-tion. Pop-u - la-tion lay to waste. See our moth-er
a - tion. Pop-u - la-tion.)

put to death.   See   our moth - er   die.

Guitar solo

Double time

3rd Verse

Smol-der-ing de-cay.   Take her breath a-way.   Mil-lions of our years   in

min-utes dis-ap-pears.____   Dark-en-ing in vain.   Dec-a-dence re-mains.

All is said and done.   Nev-er is the sun.____   Nev-er._____

Chorus

Fire.   To be-gin whip-ping dance of the dead.   Black-ened   is   the

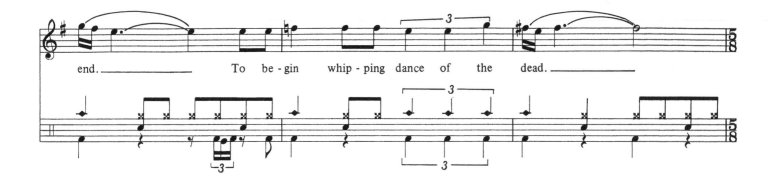

end._____ To be-gin whip-ping dance of the dead._____

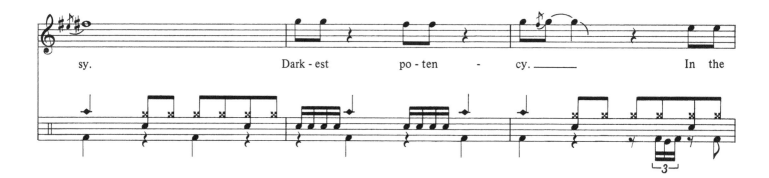

Fire is the out - come of hy - poc - ri -

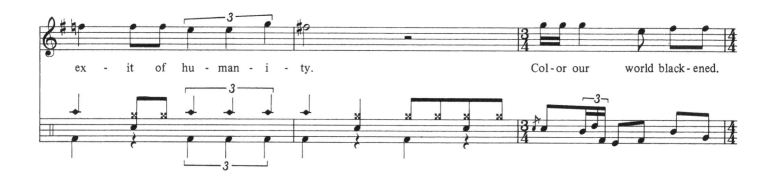

sy. Dark - est po - ten - cy. _____ In the

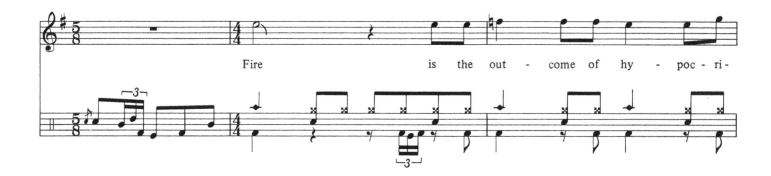

ex - it of hu - man - i - ty. Col - or our world black - ened.

Black - ened.

...AND JUSTICE FOR ALL

Words and Music by
James Hetfield, Lars Ulrich
Kirk Hammett

15

1st, 2nd, 3rd Verses

1. Halls of jus - tice paint - ed green. Mon - ey talk-ing.__
2. Ap - a - thy their step - ping stone. So un - feel-ing.__
3. La - dy jus - tice has been raped. Truth as - sas - sin.__

Pow - er wolves be - set your door, hear them stalk-ing.__
Hid - den deep an - i - mos - i - ty, so de - ceiv - ing.__
Rolls of red tape seal your lips. Now you're done in.

*3rd time cymbal line
plays ♩ on beat 2.

Soon you'll please their ap - pe - tite, they de - vour.__
through your eyes their light burns, hop - ing to find.__
Their mon - ey tips her scales a - gain. Make your deal.__

*3rd time cymbal line
plays ♩ on beat 2.

Ham - mer of jus - tice crush-es you. O - ver-pow-er.__
In - qui - si - tion seek-ing you with cry - ing__ might.
Just what is truth? I can - not tell, can - not feel.__

*3rd time cymbal line
plays ♩ on beat 2.

Play this bar 3rd time only | Pre-chorus

The ul - ti - mate__ in van-

3

16

i - ty.____ Ex - ploit - ing their_ su - prem-

a - cy.____ I can't be - lieve_ the things ___

____ you say.____ I can't be - lieve,_ I

2nd time substitute Drum Pat. 1;
3rd time substitute Drum Pat. 4

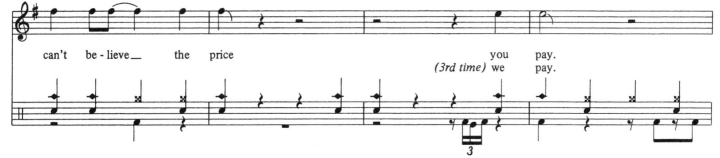

can't be - lieve___ the price   you   pay.
                    (3rd time) we pay.

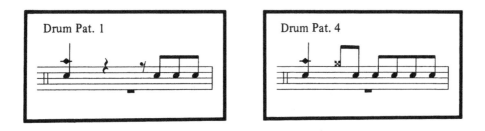

Drum Pat. 1   Drum Pat. 4

*2nd and 3rd times cymbal line plays ♩ on beat 1.

Moderately slow ♩ = 100

rit.

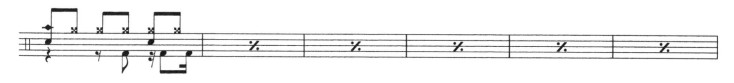

Faster ♩ = 168

Band in

D.S. al Coda

w/Drum Fig. 1 (2 times)

8

Coda

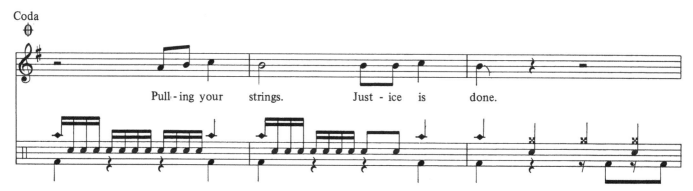

Pull-ing your   strings.   Just-ice is   done.

Seek - ing no truth. Win - ning is

all. Find it so grim, so true, so real._____

w/Drum Fig. 1 (2 times)

Seek - ing no truth. Win - ning is all. Find it so grim, so true, so real._____

*2nd time cymbal line plays on beat 1.
Play 3 times

EYE OF THE BEHOLDER

Words and Music by
James Hetfield, Lars Ulrich
and Kirk Hammett

Lim - it your i - mag - i - na - tion, keep you where they must.

2nd, 4th, 5th Verses

2. Do you feel what I___ feel?   Bit - ter - ing___ dis - tress.   Who de - cides what you___ ex - press?___
4. Do you need what I___ need?   Bound - 'ries o - ver - thrown.   Look in - side, to each___ his own.___
5. Do you know what I___ know? Your mon - ey and___ your wealth.   You si - lence just to hear___ your - self.___

2nd time substitute Drum Pat. 1;
3rd time substitute Drum Pat. 5

Do you take what I___ take?   En - dur - ance is the word.___
Do you trust what I___ trust?   Me, my - self, and I.___
Do you want what I___ want?   De - si - re not a thing.___   I

*3rd time
cymbal
line plays

Drum Pat. 1

Drum Pat. 5

Mov-ing back in-stead of for - ward seems to me ab - surd.
Pen - e - trate the smoke screen, I__ see through the self - ish lie.
hun-ger af - ter in - de - pend-ence, length - en free - dom's ring.

*2nd and 3rd times bass drum
plays on beat 4.

Does - n't mat-ter what__ you see, or in - to it what__ you read.

3rd time substitute Drum Pat. 6

Play this bar 1st time only

You can do it your__ own way, if it's done just how__ I say.

Play this bar 1st and 2nd times only

2nd time substitute Drum Pat. 2;
3rd time substitute Drum Pat. 7

*3rd time bass drum
rests on beat 4.

Drum Pat. 6

3rd Verse

Do you fear what I__ fear? Liv - ing prop - er - ly.__ Truths to you are lies_ to me.__

Do you choose what I__choose? More al - ter - na - tives.__

En - er - gy de - rives_ from both_ the plus and neg - a - tive.__

D.S. al Coda I

Coda I

D.S. al Coda II

Coda II

Free - dom of choice is made— for you, my friend!—

Free - dom of speech is words__ that they will bend!__

Free - dom with their ex - cep - tion!

Does-n't mat-ter what__ you see, or in-to it what__ you read. You can do it your__ own way,

if it's done just how__ I say!

THE SHORTEST STRAW

Words and Music by
James Hetfield and Lars Ulrich

Double time feel

1st, 2nd Verses

1. Sus - pi - cion is your_ name. Your hon - es - ty to_ blame. Put dig - ni - ty to_ shame.
2. The ac - cu - sa - tions_ fly. Dis - crim - i - na - tion,_ why? Your in - ner self to_ die.

*2nd time bass drum plays ♪ on beat 2.

Dis - hon - or.   Witch - hunt, mod - ern_ day.   De - ter - min - ing de - cay.
In - trud - ing.   Doubt sunk it - self in_ you.   Its teeth and tal - ons_ through.

2nd time substitute Drum Pat. 1

The bla - tant dis - ar - ray.   Dis - fig - ure.   The pub - lic eye's dis - grace
Your liv - ing catch two - two. De - lud - ing.   A mass hys - ter - i - a.

2nd time substitute Drum Pat. 2

De - fy - ing com - mon - place. Un - end - ing pa - per_ chase. Un - end - ing.
A meg - a - lo - man - i - a.   Re - veal de - men - ti - a.   Re - veal.

Drum Pat. 1

Drum Pat. 2

30

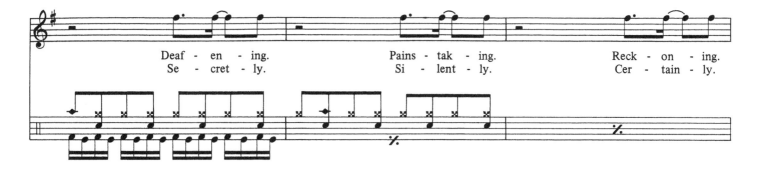

Deaf - en - ing. Pains - tak - ing. Reck - on - ing.
Se - cret - ly. Si - lent - ly. Cer - tain - ly.

2nd time substitute Drum Pat. 3

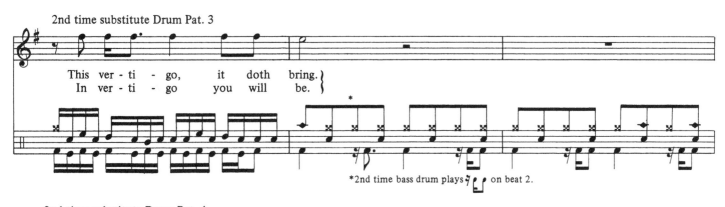

This ver - ti - go, it doth bring.
In ver - ti - go you will be.

*2nd time bass drum plays ♪ on beat 2.

2nd time substitute Drum Pat. 4

2nd time substitute Drum Pat. 5

*2nd time bass drum plays ♪ on beat 2.

Tempo I

2nd time substitute Drum Pat. 6

Chorus

Short - est straw. Chal - lenge lib - er - ty. Downed by law.

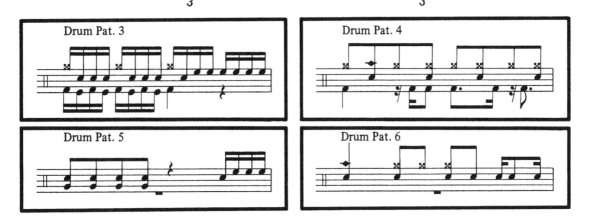

Drum Pat. 3

Drum Pat. 4

Drum Pat. 5

Drum Pat. 6

Live in in - fa - my. Rub you raw. Witch - hunt rid - ing through.

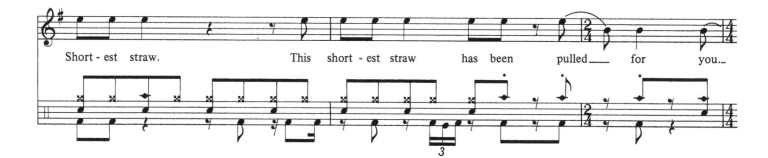

Short - est straw. This short - est straw has been pulled___ for you.__

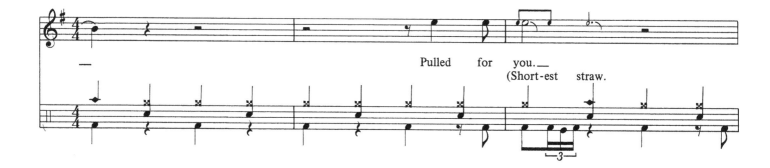

Pulled for you.___
(Short - est straw.

2nd time substitute Drum Pat. 7

Pulled for you. Pulled for
Short - est straw.

Double-time feel

you. Short - est straw has been pulled___ for you._____
Short - est straw.)

Drum Pat. 7

*2nd time bass drum plays on beat 3.

2nd time substitute Drum Pat. 8

Guitar Solo I

*2nd time cymbal line plays ⅹ ⅹ on beat 1.

Drum Pat. 8

Tempo I

(Short - est straw.   Pulled for you.   Short - est straw.   Pulled for

you.   Pulled for you.   Short - est straw has been pulled

Short - est straw.   Short - est straw.)

Guitar solo II

— for you.

Verse 3

Be - hind you, hands are tied. Your be - ing, os - tra - cized. Your hell is mul - ti - plied.

Up - end - ing. The fall - out has be - gun. Op - pres - sive dam - age_ done.

Your man - y turn to_ none. To noth - ing. You're reach - ing your na - dir.

Your will has dis - ap - peared. The lie is crys - tal_ clear. De - fend - ing.

Chan - nels_ red. One word_ said. Black - list - ed.

With ver - ti - go make you dead.

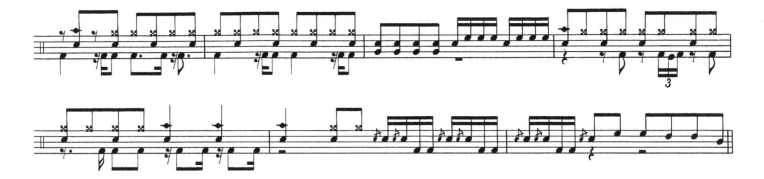

Chorus

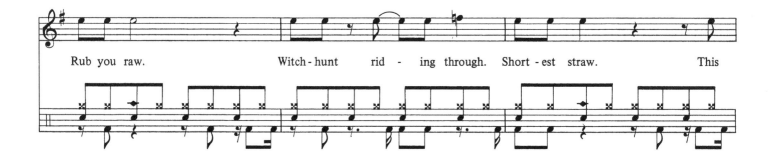

Short - est straw.   Chal - lenge lib - er - ty.   Downed by law.   Live in in - fa - my.

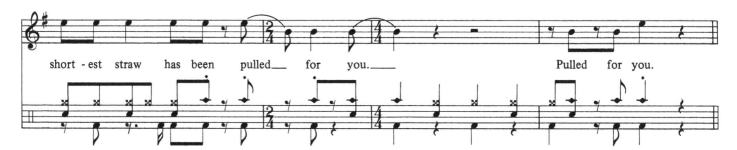

Rub you raw.   Witch - hunt rid - ing through.   Short - est straw.   This

short - est straw has been pulled___ for you.___   Pulled for you.

Double time feel

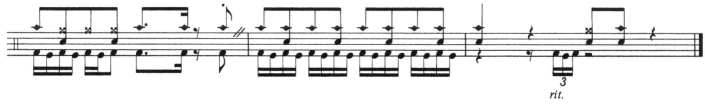

rit.

36

HARVESTER OF SORROW

Words and Music by
James Hetfield and Lars Ulrich

1st Verse

My life suf - fo - cates. Plant - ing seeds_ of hate. I've loved, turned_ to hate.

Trapped far be - yond_ my fate._ I give, you take this life that I_ for - sake.

Been cheat - ed of my_ youth. You turned this love_ to truth._____

Pre-chorus

An - ger, mis - er - y, you'll suf - fer un - to_ me.

38

Chorus

Har - vest-er___ of sor - row.___

(Lan - guage of__ the mad.)__

Har - vest-er___ of sor - row.___

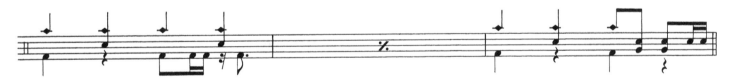

2nd Verse

Pure black look - ing clear.   My work is done_ soon_ here.   Try get - ting back_ to _ me.

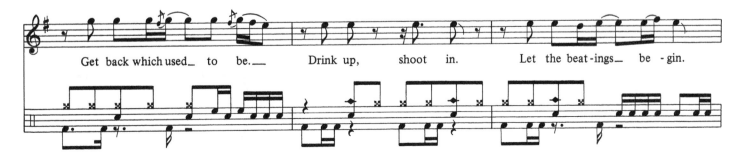

Get back which used_ to be._   Drink up,   shoot in.   Let the beat-ings_ be - gin.

Dis - trib - u - tor__ of pain. Your loss be - comes__ my gain._____

Pre-chorus

An - ger, mis - er - y, you'll suf - fer un - to__ me.

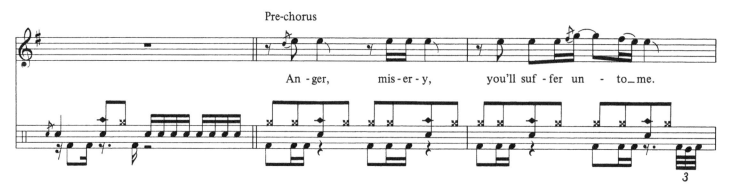

Chorus

Har - vest - er__ of sor - row.__ Har - vest - er__ of sor - row.__
(Lan - guage of__ the mad.)__

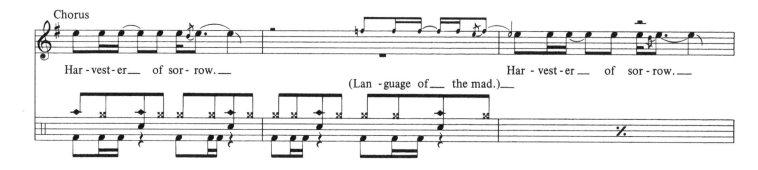

Guitar solo

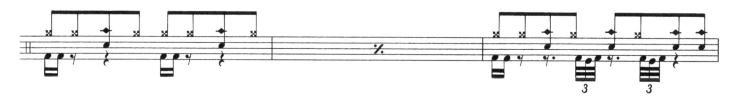

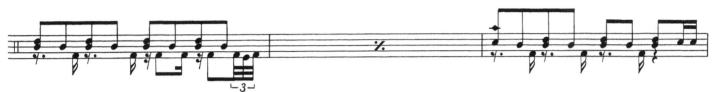

3rd Verse

All have said__ their__ pray'rs.   In -vade their__ night - mares.   To see in - to__ my__ eyes.

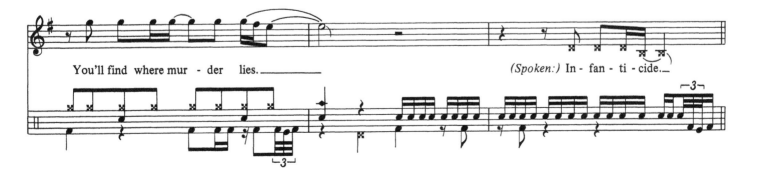

You'll find where mur - der lies._____   *(Spoken:)* In - fan - ti - cide.__

Chorus

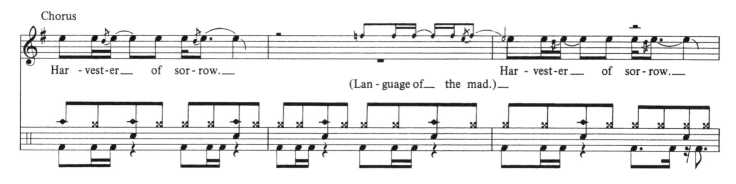

Har - vest-er__ of sor - row.__
(Lan - guage of__ the mad.)__
Har - vest-er__ of sor - row.__

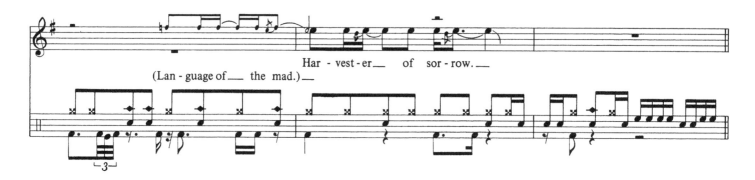

Har - vest-er__ of sor - row.__
(Lan - guage of__ the mad.)__

Har - vest-er__ of sor - row.__
Har - vest-er__ of sor - row.__

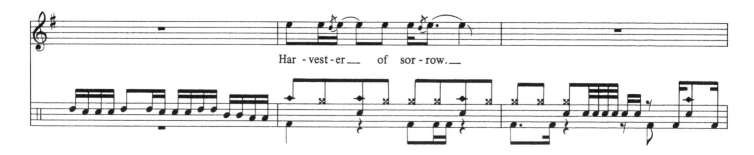

Har - vest-er__ of sor - row.__

Har - vest-er__ of sor - row.__
Har - vest-er__ of sor - row.__

TO LIVE IS TO DIE

Words and Music by
James Hetfield, Lars Ulrich
and Cliff Burton

43

44

*2nd time snare plays ♩ ; bass drum rests on beat 1.

poco rit.-- rit.--

(Spoken:) When a man   lies, he murders some part of the

world.   These are the pale deaths which men miscall their   lives.   All   this I cannot

bear   to   witness   any   longer.   Cannot   the   kingdom of salvation take me home?

*2nd time cymbal line plays ⅹ on beat 1.

*Acoustic guitar enters at ♩ = 56.

Play 3 times   Begin fade

Fade out*

*Acoustic guitar continues for approx.
20 seconds. *Segue to "Dyers Eve"*

DYERS EVE

Words and Music by
James Hetfield, Lars Ulrich
and Kirk Hammett

1st, 2nd, 3rd Verses

1. Dear Moth - er, dear Fa - ther.___   What is this___ hell you___
2. Dear Moth - er, dear Fa - ther.___   Time has fro - zen still___
3. Dear Moth - er, dear Fa - ther.___   Hid - den in___ your world

___ have put___ me through? Be - liev - er, de - ceiv - er.___
___ what's left___ to be. Hear noth - ing, say noth - ing.___
___ you've made_ for me. I'm seeth - ing, I'm bleed - ing.___

Day in, day___ out, live___ my life___ for you. Pushed on - to me what's wrong
Can - not face_ the fact_ I think_ for me. No guar - an - tee, it's life___
Rip - ping wounds_ in me___ that nev - er heal. Un - dy - ing spite I feel

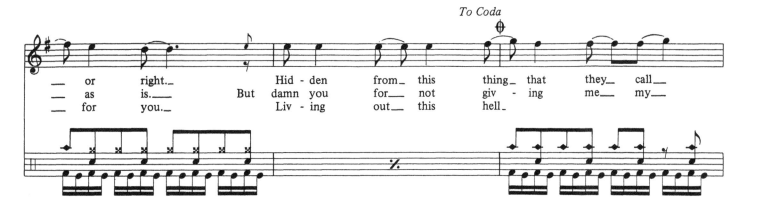

To Coda

— or right.— / — as is.— / — for you.—

But damn you for not giv - ing me— my— / Liv - ing out— this hell—

Hid - den from— this thing— that they— call—

2nd time substitute Drum Pat. 1

life. / chance.

Dear Moth - er, dear Fa - ther.— / Dear Moth - er, dear Fa - ther.—

Ev - 'ry thought— I'd think— / You clipped my wings— be - fore—

— you'd dis - ap -prove. / — I learned— to fly.

Cur - a - tor, dic - ta - tor.— / Un - spoiled, un - spo - ken.—

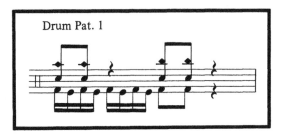

Drum Pat. 1

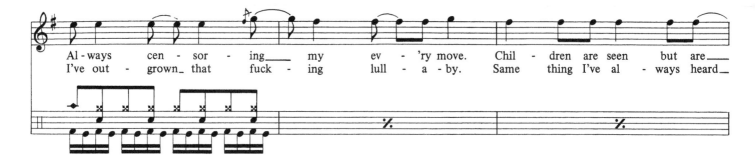

Al - ways cen - sor - ing___ my ev - 'ry move. Chil - dren are seen but are___
I've out - grown_ that fuck - ing lull - a - by. Same thing I've al - ways heard___

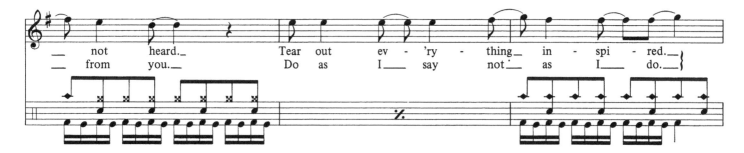

___ not heard._ Tear out ev - 'ry - thing_ in - spi - red._
___ from you._ Do as I_ say not_ as I_ do._

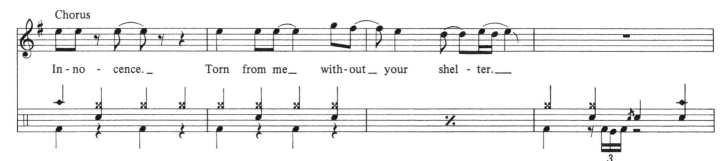

Chorus

In - no - cence._ Torn from me_ with - out_ your shel - ter._

Barred re - al - i - ty.___ I'm liv - ing blind - ly._____

Moderate Rock ♩ = 168

Bridge

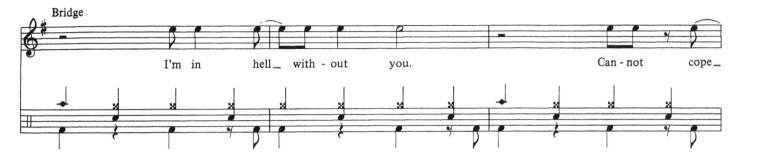

I'm in hell_ with - out you. Can - not cope_

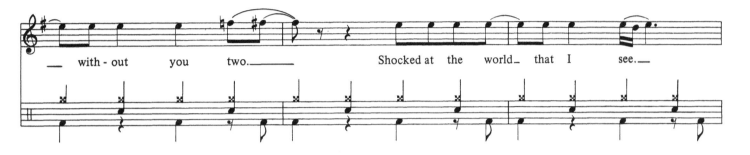

_ with - out you two._____ Shocked at the world_ that I see.__

In - no - cent vic - tim, please res - cue__ me.

D.S. al Coda

Coda

_ you al - ways_ knew.

THE FRAYED ENDS OF SANITY

Words and Music by
James Hetfield, Lars Ulrich
and Kirk Hammett

*Backwards recorded cymbal swell.

1st Verse
Double-time feel   Half-time feel

Nev-er hun-ger.   Nev-er pros - per.   I have fall - en prey to fail - ure.____

Double-time feel

Strug - gle with-in   trig - gered a - gain.   Now the can-dle burns at both ends.___

Half-time feel   Double-time feel   Half-time feel

Twist - ing un - der schiz - o - phre - nia.___

Double-time feel   Half-time feel

Fall - ing deep in - to de - men - tia.___

Double time feel

Chorus

Old hab - its re - ap - pear.＿ Fight - ing＿ the fear of fear.＿

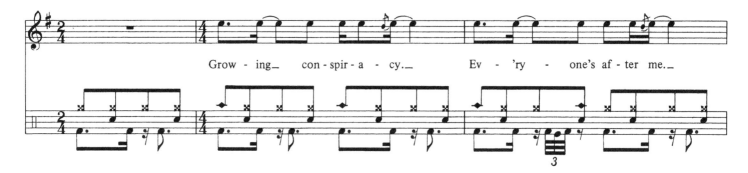

Grow - ing＿ con - spir - a - cy.＿ Ev - 'ry - one's af - ter me.＿

Frayed ends＿ of san - i - ty.＿ Hear them call - ing,＿ hear them call - ing

me.＿＿＿＿＿

2nd, 3rd Verses
Double time feel

2nd time substitute Drum Pat. 1

2. Birth of ter - ror.   Death of much more.   I'm the slave of fear, my cap - tor.
3. In - to ruin   I am sink - ing.   Hos-tage of this name - less feel - ing.

Half time feel

Double time feel

Nev - er warn - ings,   spread - ing its wings   as I wait for the hor - ror she brings.
Hell is set free,   flood - ed I'll be,   feel the un - der - tow in - side me.

Half time feel
2nd time substitute Drum Pat. 2

Double time feel

Loss of in - t'rest, ques - tion, won - der.
Height, hell, time, haste, ter - ror, ten - sion.

Drum Pat. 1

Drum Pat. 2

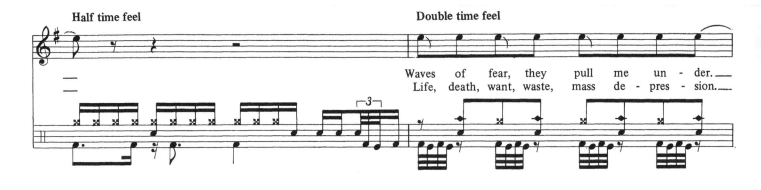

Half time feel   **Double time feel**

Waves of fear, they pull me un - der.___
Life, death, want, waste, mass de - pres - sion.___

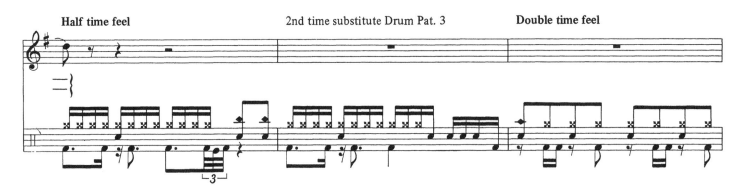

Half time feel   2nd time substitute Drum Pat. 3   **Double time feel**

2nd time substitute Drum Pat. 4

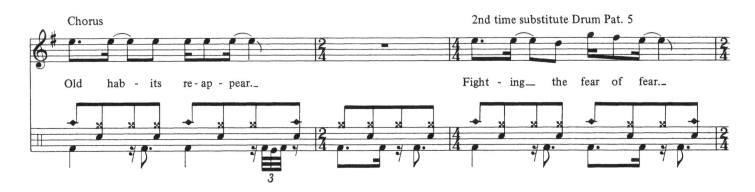

Chorus   2nd time substitute Drum Pat. 5

Old hab - its re - ap - pear.___   Fight - ing___ the fear of fear.___

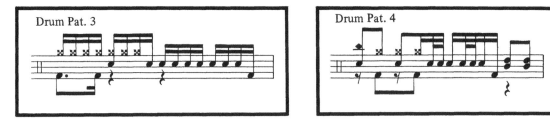

Drum Pat. 3

Drum Pat. 4

Drum Pat. 5

Grow - ing_ con -spir-a - cy.__ Ev - 'ry - one's af - ter me.__
(2nd time) My - self_ is af - ter me.__

Frayed ends_ of san - i - ty.__ Hear them call - ing,__ hear them call - ing

me.__

Double time ♩ = 192   *Play 4 times*

*2nd, 3rd and 4th times cymbal line plays ✗ beat 1.

Play 4 times

Guitar solo

Half time ♩ = 96

D.S. al Coda

Coda

Frayed ends_ of san-i-ty._ Hear them call - ing. Frayed ends_ of san-i-ty._

Hear them call - ing,_____ hear them call - ing

Double time ♩ = 192
Outro

me._____ Ah ha ha ha.___

ONE

Words and Music by
James Hetfield and Lars Ulrich

*Battlefield sound effects for approx. 15 sec.

1st Verse

me! _____

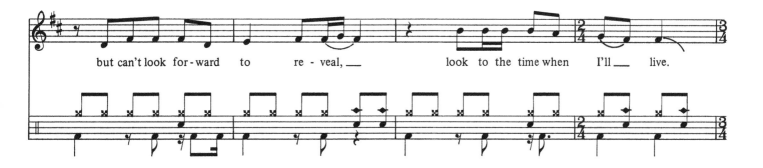

2nd Verse

Back in the womb it's much   too real, ___   in pumps life that   I   must ___ feel,

but can't look for - ward   to   re - veal, ___   look to the time when   I'll ___   live.

Fed through the tube that sticks   in me, ___   just like a war - time nov - el - ty;

tied to mach-ines that make me be. ___ Cut this life off from ___ me!

Hold my breath as I wish for death. ___ Oh please God, wake

me! _____

Now the world is gone, I'm just one. ___ Oh God, help me.

Hold my breath as I wish for death.___ Oh please God, help me!___

Darkness im - pris - on - ing me, all that I see, ab - so - lute hor - ror!
Land - mine has tak - en my sight, tak - en my speech, tak - en my hear - ing,

2nd time substitute Drum Fig. 1

I can - not live! I can - not die! Trapped in my - self, bod - y my hold - ing
tak - en my arms, tak - en my legs, tak - en my soul, left me with life in

1.
cell! ____

2. **Double time**
hell! ____
(Sing 1st time only)

*2nd time bass drum plays on beat 3.

*2nd time bass drums play on beat 3.

Drum Fig. 1

Guitar solo

*2nd time play snare
and crash on beat 4.

71

Play 4 times

*Play crash 1st time only;
2nd, 3rd, 4th time play hi-hat.

*4th time bass drums play
on beat 3; snare plays
flam on beat 4.